Albert Einstein™

A BOOK OF POSTCARDS

POMEGRANATE ARTBOOKS
SAN FRANCISCO

Pomegranate Artbooks
Box 6099
Rohnert Park, CA 94927

Pomegranate Europe Ltd.
Fullbridge House, Fullbridge
Maldon, Essex CM9 7LE
England

ISBN 0-7649-0041-2
Pomegranate Catalog No. A873

Pomegranate publishes books of
postcards on a wide range of subjects.
Please write to the publisher for more information.

Designed by Thomas Morley and Mark Koenig
Printed in Korea

05 04 03 02 01 00 99 98 97 10 9 8 7 6 5 4 3 2

Albert Einstein (1879–1955), one of the greatest theoretical physicists of all time, revolutionized the world of modern physics. An individual of monumental intellectual achievement, he remains the most influential theoretical physicist of the modern era. To this day Einstein receives popular recognition unprecedented for a scientist. Yet his humanity—his humility, simplicity, compassion, and humor—is as important as his intellect. Einstein's reverence for all creation; his deep concern with the social impact of scientific discovery; his belief in the grandeur, beauty, and sublimity of the universe (the primary source of inspiration in his science); and his feelings of awe for the scheme manifested in the material universe permeated his work and philosophy. Despite his unfathomable genius, his monumental contributions to scientific theory, and his unswerving dedication to matters humane, Einstein remained a humble, approachable man throughout his life, finding joy in simple pleasures and cherishing his solitude. "The ideals that have lighted my way, and time after time have given me new courage to face life cheerfully, have been Kindness, Beauty, and Truth," he said. "A hundred times every day I remind myself that my inner and outer lives are based on the labors of other men, living and dead." The thirty photographs presented here provide an intimate glimpse of the human side of this great scientist. All are from the book *Essential Einstein* (Pomegranate Artbooks, 1995).

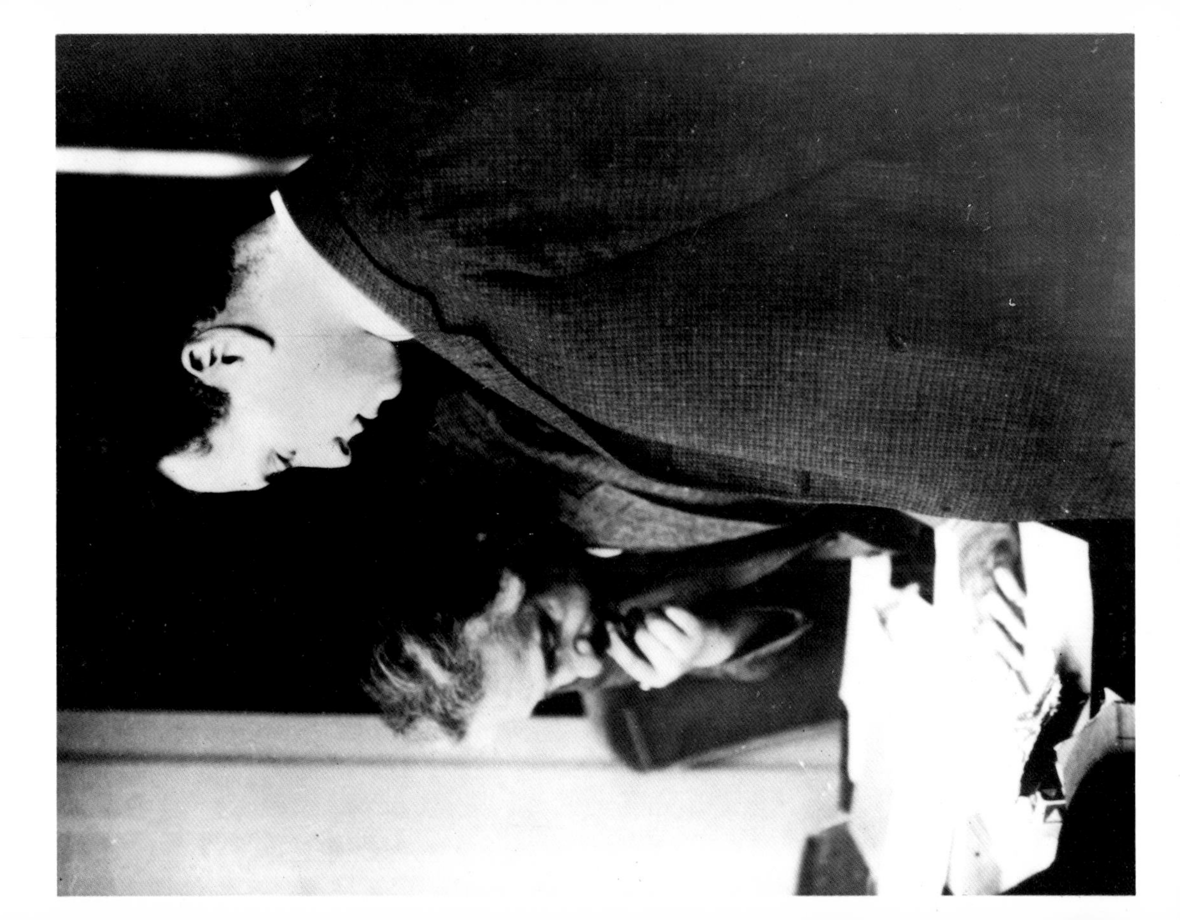

Albert Einstein™ (1879–1955)

Albert Einstein with American physicist Wolfgang Pauli, 1926

Pomegranate, Box 6099, Rohnert Park, CA 94927

Albert Einstein™ (1879–1955)

Albert Einstein, 1912

Pomegranate, Box 6099, Rohnert Park, CA 94927

Photograph by J. F. Langhans, courtesy The Hebrew University of Jerusalem, Israel

Albert Einstein™ (1879–1955)

Albert Einstein with American physicist J. R. Oppenheimer at the Institute for Advanced Study, 1947

Pomegranate, Box 6099, Rohnert Park, CA 94927

Photograph courtesy AIP Niels Bohr Library

Albert Einstein™ (1879–1955)

Albert Einstein, 1935

Pomegranate, Box 6099, Rohnert Park, CA 94927

Photograph courtesy Library of Congress

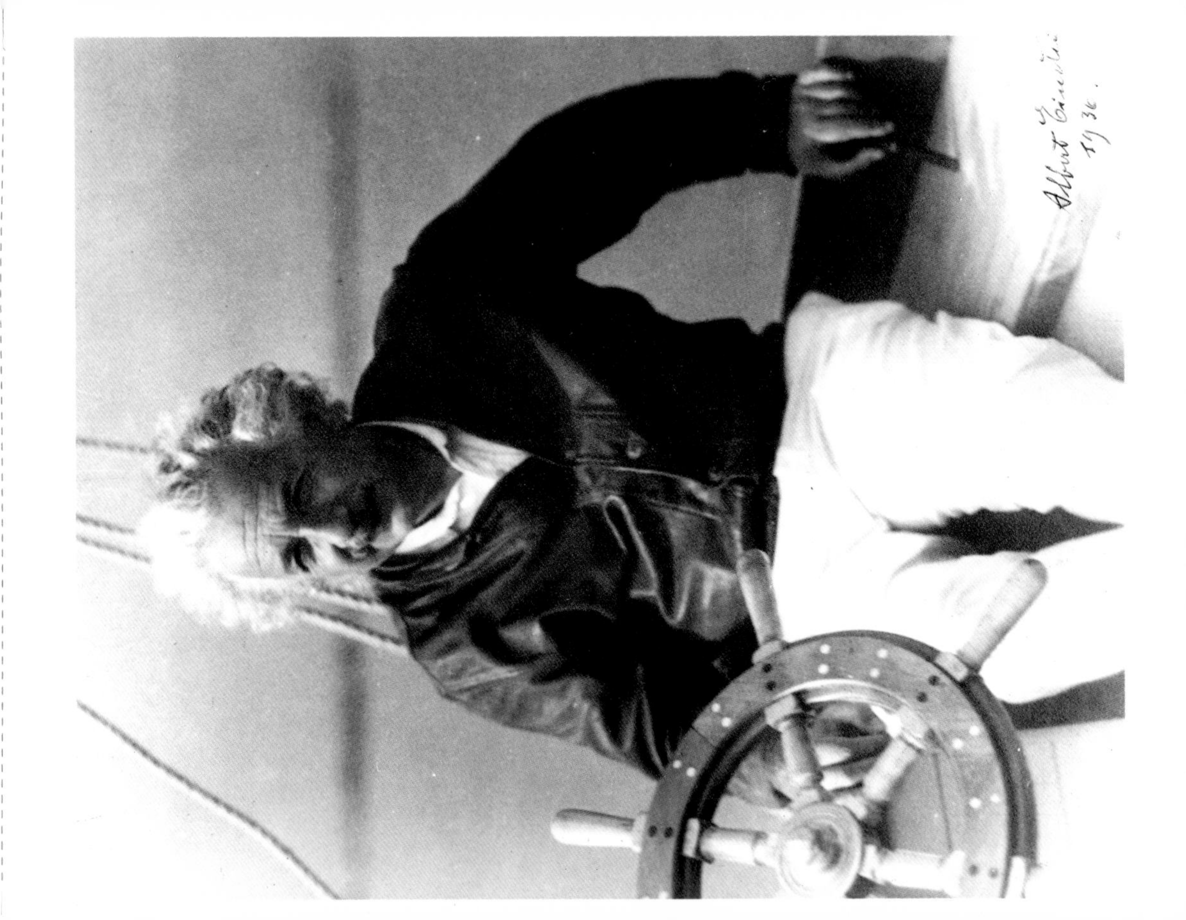

Albert Einstein™ (1879–1955)

Albert Einstein sailing, 1936

Pomegranate, Box 6099, Rohnert Park, CA 94927

Photograph courtesy AIP Niels Bohr Library

Albert Einstein™ (1879–1955)

Pomegranate, Box 6099, Rohnert Park, CA 94927

Albert Einstein™ (1879–1955)

Albert Einstein and his wife, Elsa, Saranac Lake, New York, n.d.

Pomegranate, Box 6099, Rohnert Park, CA 94927

Albert Einstein™ (1879–1955)

Albert Einstein, 1933

Pomegranate, Box 6099, Rohnert Park, CA 94927

Photograph courtesy AIP Niels Bohr Library

Albert Einstein™ (1879–1955)

Albert Einstein in Berlin, December 1932

Pomegranate, Box 6099, Rohnert Park, CA 94927

Photograph by Charles Holdt, courtesy AIP Niels Bohr Library

Albert Einstein™ (1879–1955)

Pomegranate, Box 6099, Rohnert Park, CA 94927

Photograph courtesy Leo Baeck Institute, New York

Albert Einstein™ (1879–1955)
Albert Einstein at home in Caputh, Germany, c. 1931

Pomegranate, Box 6099, Rohnert Park, CA 94927

Albert Einstein™ (1879–1955)

D. H. Menzel, Albert Einstein, American mathematician George Birkhoff, and American astronomer Harlow Shapley's son, Carl, at the time of Einstein's receiving an honorary degree from Harvard University, Cambridge, Massachusetts, 1935

Pomegranate, Box 6099, Rohnert Park, CA 94927

Albert Einstein™ (1879–1955)

Albert Einstein in Caputh, Germany, October 1929

Pomegranate, Box 6099, Rohnert Park, CA 94927

Photograph courtesy Leo Baeck Institute, New York

Albert Einstein™ (1879–1955)

Albert Einstein's secretary, Helen Dukas; Albert Einstein; and Margot Einstein taking the U.S. oath of allegiance, 1940

Pomegranate, Box 6099, Rohnert Park, CA 94927

Photograph courtesy AIP Niels Bohr Library

Albert Einstein™ (1879–1955)

Albert Einstein and Elsa with others at a tea ceremony,
Japan, 1922

Pomegranate, Box 6099, Rohnert Park, CA 94927

Albert Einstein™ (1879–1955)

Albert Einstein with German chemist Fritz Haber, n.d.

Pomegranate, Box 6099, Rohnert Park, CA 94927

Albert Einstein™ (1879–1955)

Albert Einstein with baby John Steidig, Deep Creek Lake, Maryland, c. 1946

Pomegranate, Box 6099, Rohnert Park, CA 94927

Albert Einstein™ (1879–1955)

Dutch physicist Pieter Zeeman, Albert Einstein, and Austrian physicist Paul Ehrenfest in Zeeman's laboratory, Amsterdam, n.d.

Pomegranate, Box 6099, Rohnert Park, CA 94927

Photograph by Ruhl Studios, courtesy The Hebrew University of Jerusalem, Israel

Albert Einstein™ (1879–1955)

Pomegranate, Box 6099, Rohnert Park, CA 94927

Albert Einstein™ (1879–1955)

Pomegranate, Box 6099, Rohnert Park, CA 94927

Photograph courtesy Leo Baeck Institute, New York

Albert Einstein™ (1879–1955)

Albert Einstein with Austrian physicist Paul Ehrenfest and Dutch astronomer Willelm de Sitter (back row) and English astronomer Arthur Eddington and Dutch physicist Hendrik Lorentz (front row), Leiden, Netherlands

Pomegranate, Box 6099, Rohnert Park, CA 94927

Albert Einstein™ (1879–1955)

Albert Einstein in middle age. Engraving by Rose Weiser. Photographische Gesellschaft, Berlin, n.d.

Pomegranate, Box 6099, Rohnert Park, CA 94927

Albert Einstein™ (1879–1955)

Albert Einstein with American electrical engineer C. P. Steinmetz, c. 1920s

Pomegranate, Box 6099, Rohnert Park, CA 94927

Albert Einstein™ (1879–1955)

Albert Einstein with Rabindranath Tagore, Berlin

Pomegranate, Box 6099, Rohnert Park, CA 94927

Photograph courtesy The Hebrew University of Jerusalem, Israel

Albert Einstein™ (1879–1955)

Albert Einstein, Pasadena, California, c. 1930

Pomegranate, Box 6099, Rohnert Park, CA 94927

Photograph courtesy The Hebrew University of Jerusalem, Israel

© SCHLOSS
1.

Albert Einstein™ (1879–1955)

Albert Einstein, n.d.

Pomegranate, Box 6099, Rohnert Park, CA 94927

Photograph courtesy Library of Congress

Albert Einstein™ (1879–1955)

Albert Einstein with Z. Gezari in Albert Einstein's backyard, Princeton, New Jersey, May 1954

Pomegranate, Box 6099, Rohnert Park, CA 94927

Photograph courtesy AIP Niels Bohr Library

Albert Einstein™ (1879–1955)

Albert Einstein, c. 1950

Pomegranate, Box 6099, Rohnert Park, CA 94927

Albert Einstein™ (1879–1955)

Albert Einstein, Leiden, Netherlands, 1923

Pomegranate, Box 6099, Rohnert Park, CA 94927

Photograph by Gerhard H. Dieke, courtesy AIP Niels Bohr Library

4029

Albert Einstein™ (1879–1955)

Pomegranate, Box 6099, Rohnert Park, CA 94927